FROM CHAOS TO CENTER

Additional Resources by

Aiki Works, Thomas Crum, and Judith Warner

Books:

Journey to Center, Thomas Crum (Simon & Schuster)
The Magic of Conflict, Thomas Crum (Simon & Schuster)
Your Conflict Cookbook: A Teacher's Handbook for Helping Students Deal with Anger and Conflict, Thomas Crum and Judith Warner

Videos:

The Energizer, Thomas Crum
Creative Resolution of Conflict, Thomas Crum
The Magic of Conflict, Thomas Crum (Career Track)
Violence: Dealing with Anger, Thomas Crum

Other:

The Magic of Conflict Video Seminar Kit, Thomas Crum
The Magic of Conflict Personal Guidance System, Thomas Crum
Your Journey to Center: A Personal Journal
Aiki Centering Bell
Music by Ellen Stapenhorst:
All of My Skies
Invisible Threads
The Dance

FROM CHAOS TO CENTER

A TRAINING GUIDE IN THE ART OF CENTERING

Judith S. Warner

Manufactured in the United States of America

Aiki Works, Inc.

P.O. Box 251, Victor, NY 14564
716-924-7302 • Fax: 716-924-2799

P.O. Box 7845, Aspen, CO 81612
970-925-7099 • Fax: 970-925-4532

www.aikiworks.com

Cover photo by Don Cole Harvey

ISBN 1-877803-10-3
Library of Congress Catalog Card Number: 99-90011

For Jerry, Leslie Jaye, and Mark

Contents

Acknowledgments

This book would not have been possible without the support of many people.

Special thanks to Thomas Crum, creator of the Magic of Conflict approach, who is my mentor, friend, and partner in this work;

Cathryn Crum, Ellen Stapenhorst, Jeff Finesilver, and all the other members of the Aiki Works extended family who have shared in my journey;

Shuji Maruyama Sensei and my other instructors who have patiently guided me in Kokikai Ryu Aikido;

Alyce Adams for her faithful and talented editing of my musings;

Eileen Kuchta for her steadfast encouragement and friendship;

Most of all, gratitude to my spouse, Jerry, and my children, Leslie Jaye and Mark, for their love, patience, and countless opportunities to train in the art of centering.

Introduction

For over a decade I have worked with Thomas Crum, author of *The Magic of Conflict* and *Journey to Center,* in his Magic of Conflict workshops. Tom is the quintessential workshop leader. Everyone in his programs experiences centering, regardless of background, skeptical attitudes, or learning style.

However, experiencing center in a workshop is only the tip of the iceberg. One of the most frequently asked questions in our programs is "So, how do I get centered when I leave here?"

Developing your ability to center is a lifetime pursuit. The more often you choose to center in your daily life, the more likely you will unconsciously choose a centered state in times of stress. This is our desired objective — to be centered under pressure. Since very few of us can devote a lifetime exclusively to centering training, the best way to achieve our objective is to incorporate training naturally into daily activities.

This book offers suggestions on how to train. By tailoring these guidelines to your personal lifestyle, you can create your own personal centering program.

Have fun!

Part One

The Art of Centering

What Is Center?

Center is a state of being. You are centered when you are moving on purpose, without irritation or frustration. You are centered when you are open to discovery, no matter what the circumstances, when you are willing to learn and to change based on what you learn.

Center is a mind/body state. Your body pulsates, free of tension, able to move gracefully and appropriately. Your mind is alert — with a heightened awareness of surroundings and an uncanny ability to focus on essentials.

Center is magical. It makes living effortless. It is a place of peak performance and personal satisfaction. You are entirely present in the moment and you are of greatest service to others. You are truth, integrity, honor, compassion, and joy. Centering is a gift — to you and to those around you.

Centering is "the zone" spoken of by great athletes. It can also be a barefoot run on the grass on a summer's eve, with the wind in your face and the senses wide open ... It is like a delicate flower growing out of solid rock. Center can be a cosmic laugh rippling out to the ends of the universe. It can be simply relaxing in rush-hour traffic. Center is returning home. It is always a choice we can make.

Thomas Crum

I know I am *centered* when ...

- I am balanced and stable.
- I am breathing deeply from my belly.
- I am relaxed, calm, and focused.
- I am aware, internally and externally.
- I am appreciative of myself and others.
- I am feeling my emotions — and learning from them.
- I am compassionate and connected to others and to my environment.
- I am able to receive and give sincere acknowledgment.
- I am energized by purpose.
- I am bigger than my challenges.
- I am unattached to the outcome of a situation.
- I am having fun and laughing often.

Journey to Center, Thomas Crum

How often are you centered? You have been there hundreds, maybe thousands, of times in your lifetime, but you probably are most aware of when you have been uncentered.

For some of us, it seems that we spend most of our lives in an uncentered state, just getting by, trying to deal with the stress and strain of studying, parenting, growing up, working — or even, remarkably, dealing with the stress of playing.

What would it be like if we could turn our lives around so that we are centered almost all the time, making those times when we are off-center stand out as aberrations?

You can choose center anywhere, anytime. Often, we do not recognize center as a state of being that we can choose — we think it is simply something that happens to us due to circumstances out of our control. You may recognize that you were centered at the moment you exchanged your wedding vows, or received your diploma, or scored a winning goal. From this you might conclude that a special relationship or successful achievement is necessary for centering. The truth is that those external forces support centering, but are not essential. The potential to be centered is inside us all the time.

Recognizing Center

To choose center, we must recognize it. We each categorize center in a unique way — as a kinesthetic feeling, a sound, a color. All that matters is that *you* recognize *your* centered state of being.

To increase your familiarity with your experience of the centered state, use this exercise introduced in *The Magic of Conflict* and used in all of our workshops:[1]

- Stand easily and naturally, with your feet approximately shoulder width apart.
- Have a partner stand beside you, facing in the same direction so that you feel she is there to support you, not compete with you.
- Have your partner reach over and place the fingertips of one hand very lightly just above the center of your chest.

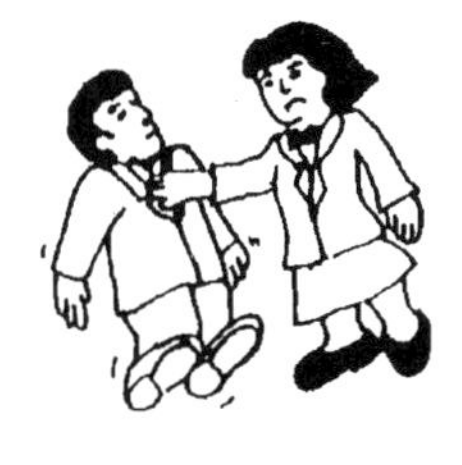

- Very slowly and smoothly your partner should increase the pressure on that point, as if she were going to push you directly back. This should be done smoothly, with no jerky or sudden motion. Stand naturally and do not try to physically resist this pressure.
- You will soon begin to wobble. Confirm with your partner how little pressure it took for this to occur.
- With your partner's fingertips in the same position on your chest, concentrate on your center — the physical center of your body — which, in a standing position, is located roughly a couple of inches below the navel. Touching that area with your finger will help you to focus your mind on the location.

- Have your partner slowly increase the pressure again, without distracting your thoughts away from your center. Take any feeling of pressure on the chest down to your center, to actually feel it "from your center."
- As your partner slowly increases the pressure on your chest, she will find that there is remarkably more stability, gained simply by you becoming more aware of your natural center. You will probably not realize how hard she is pressing.

Take time to play with this exercise. Repeat it so you begin to distinguish between centered and uncentered states, and notice what a centered experience is like for you — kinesthetically, psychologically, and sensually.

Resource Tip

Throughout this book I refer to many of the resources that Aiki Works has created over the years. For over a decade we have taught the art of centering. One of the many support materials we have prepared is a video, *The Energizer*, featuring Thomas Crum. This video provides a visual demonstration of the basic centering exercise described above, which you may find helpful.

Embrace Center

Once you recognize center, you can begin to train in it. At first this requires trust. Do not expect major breakthroughs to happen daily. Let go of attachment to measurable outcomes. Persist in your training. Appreciate your moments of centeredness. Take in everything about your world at these times, and persist in your training. With time, centeredness will become akin to a familiar hearth where you can rest your weary bones and revitalize yourself.

Embracing center is acknowledging yourself. Centering allows you to experience your emotions without being dominated by them. It supports congruency between your values and your actions. If you live your life at this level, you come to not only know yourself very well, but to accept and appreciate who you are. This is a powerful place to be.

I looked in a mirror and saw my soul.
And I smiled.

Centering Moment

The founder of the martial art of Aikido, Morihei Ueshiba, was asked if he was centered all the time, for to his students, it appeared that he was.

Ueshiba responded that he lost center continually, but he regained it so quickly that no one ever noticed.

Part Two

Training Themes

Centering Training

There is no right or wrong way to train in centering. Visualize your life before you as unmarked territory, your path to center not yet known. Your journey will be uniquely yours, shaped by your needs and preferences.

Our purpose is to provide some guideposts to help you on your journey. In this book, and in our Aiki Works workshops, centering exercises and suggestions revolved around five main themes. If you integrate training elements from each of these themes into your life, your ability to center under pressure will increase dramatically.

Within each theme you will find a myriad of suggestions and examples. Many come from our workshops. Others have worked for me in my own training. Don't feel limited to the tips in the pages that follow. They are not intended to be comprehensive, but rather to provide direction, to inspire you to try them and to develop your own unique ideas.

The Five Themes of Centering Training

The Breath

Reinforcements

Reflection

Vision

Support Systems

Theme One
The Breath

Breathing is natural — for everyone! You can use your breath as a means to center. Whenever you are aware of tension in your body, turn breathing into your ally by breathing deeply and slowly from your abdomen. The key is to take *deep* slow breaths.

Many of us breathe shallowly much of the time. When we are tense, we breathe faster, using even less of our lung capacity. We need to reverse this pattern to have our breath support us in returning to center.

In our week-long workshops we begin each day with a period of meditation and breath exercises such as misogi breathing. In a few short days of regular practice, workshop participants notice a change in their dispositions. They are lighter, happier, and more relaxed, despite the intensive study in some of our programs.

When breath work is incorporated into your daily rituals, it is available to support you in times of stress, whenever you experience life closing in on you.

Misogi Breathing

This process may be done in a traditional meditative position such as seiza or the lotus position, or while simply seated in a chair. Sit slightly forward in the chair, your feet flat on the floor, your hands resting on your thighs. Inhale slowly through your nose until your lungs feel full. You will feel your belly expand as you fill your lungs. Pause. Exhale through your mouth, making the sound of Ah-h-h, emptying your lungs totally and gently contracting your abdominal muscles. Pause, then repeat the cycle.

The inhalation/exhalation cycle is done at a slow, even tempo comfortable for you. You do not want to find yourself gasping for air at any point in the cycle. This exercise is not about scarcity, or a perception of it. Rather, it is designed to nurture your body and spirit with the abundance of the universe. As you discover your appropriate pace, you learn about your body and its abilities and constraints.

Visualization is an integral part of misogi breathing. As you inhale, see and feel support and energy filling your body. With each exhalation, visualize letting go, releasing tension, and sending positive thoughts to the universe. Inhalation leads to exhalation, exhalation leads to inhalation. The flow of the breath becomes one with the flow of the mind. You are merged into a greater whole than yourself, while maintaining your own integrity.

With practice, misogi breathing becomes natural. You will automatically enter a centered state as you breathe.

Resource Tip

The Energizer video by Thomas Crum provides a visual demonstration of misogi breathing.

Breathing Moments

• Create times in each day when you take notice of your breathing. You may pick a repetitious daily activity, such as washing the dishes. Resolve that you will simply hold an awareness of your breath as you perform the task.

• In those moments when you are "on hold" — waiting in line, sitting in traffic, waiting for your computer to boot up or complete a Web connection — observe your breathing. Take long, deep breaths. Stretch your body, however briefly, and then continue on with the flow of your life.

• When working with children and teens, we often refer to an exercise called Breathe Five. Students are instructed to inhale and exhale to a count of five when they are experiencing frustration or anger. Develop this practice for yourself.

Whenever you are feeling stressed, count to five with a deep breath and then slowly exhale to a count of five, before you say or do anything.

Centering Moment

Set aside a particular time each day for your breathing practice. Ten to twenty minutes is ideal. If you begin your day this way, you will find yourself better prepared to embrace the world and give yourself fully to your daily tasks. If you choose to close your day with a few minutes of breathing, your sleep will be more restful.

Choosing a Smile

The Vietnamese monk Thich Nhat Hanh writes extensively about breath work and meditation. He often refers to smiling in his writings: "During walking meditation, during kitchen and garden work, during sitting meditation, all day long we can practice smiling. At first you may find it difficult to smile, and we have to think about why. Smiling means that we are ourselves, that we are not drowned into forgetfulness." [2]

He offers this short poem to say periodically while breathing and smiling:

Breathing in, I calm my body.
Breathing out, I smile.
Dwelling in the present moment
I know this is a wonderful moment.[3]

Just imagine if you simply took some time each day to consciously smile. What would happen if, in the midst of a crisis, when you think things are at their worst, you were to pause, take a deep breath, and smile. It sounds crazy, but I've done it. My experience is that it lightens the air, my stomach relaxes, and something clicks within that challenges me to find a perspective that takes the melodrama out of the event, and instead brings a positive mindfulness.

Breath is the bridge which connects life to consciousness; which unites your body to your thoughts. Whenever your mind becomes scattered, use your breath as the means to take hold of your mind again.

Thich Nhat Hanh

Present Moment

Breathing can transform moments of fear into centering training. We hold our breath for many reasons — surprise, anger, stillness, and fear. Fear is an uncentered state. Whether a simple worry over our performance or adequacy, or terror over potential catastrophe, fear is a very real and paralyzing state of being.

When we are fearful, we are almost always focusing upon either a past event or a future possibility. We are not living in the present moment, and this is not productive in addressing the real issues. For example, I can worry about my company downsizing, or I can focus upon the moment, performing my job conscientiously and taking other steps that can prepare me for a potential reentry into the job market.

When you are fearful, notice your breathing. As you inhale, imagine support entering your body; as you exhale, visualize your panic leaving. Appreciate your centered state as you become aware of it. From this place of calmness, ask what actions you can take now to address the issue causing the upset. Focus upon those actions. This will help you to stay centered in the present moment.

Repeat this practice whenever you experience fear. Over time you will develop a pattern of action which arises from personal power in frightening times. The realization that you *are* capable of dealing with adversity is invaluable in creating a life of power and joy.

Centering Moment

Imagine you are the wind. As you breathe, see yourself traveling through this world as the wind moves. Let the ebb and flow of your breath carry you. Visit those places that are sacred to you. Rekindle the love and the peace that they nurture within you. Bask in the joy of a beautiful sunset, exclaim in awe at the majesty of a vista of mountaintops. And, know as you experience this world, that your center is its center. As you inhale, feel your core of being, acknowledge your relationship to the whole. You are one with the universe.

In your heart and your spirit, let the breezes surround you.
Lift up your voice then and sing with the wind.

John Denver

Theme Two: Reinforcements

How often have you chosen a new goal, only to abandon it because it adds even more tasks into your already overburdened calendar? When you pursue your training through centering reinforcements, you can avoid this common pitfall. These reinforcements provide you with a means for transforming ordinary moments and ordinary tasks you are already performing into centering opportunities. There is no added time commitment, only added balance.

Two basic categories of reinforcements are described in this section. *Anchors* are designated objects, words, or sounds that act as signals to remind you to return to center. *Energy extension* happens when you let your personal energy flow and expand. This is a skill you can develop, which will help you perform everyday tasks in a way that enhances your centered state.

Centering is a choice we always can make.
Thomas Crum

ANCHORS

You can use a vast array of reminders, or anchors, to reinforce your choice to center. Whenever you see a particular object or person, hear a certain sound, speak a special phrase, or enter a designated place, you can choose to center. You may quickly lose your center again, but that is okay. The object is to create a pattern of choosing center repeatedly during the day. If you follow this process, you will begin to find yourself unconsciously assuming a centered state in times of stress.

Checkpoints

Checkpoints are people or objects (and the sounds associated with them) that signal you back to center. For example, the door to your office can serve as a centering checkpoint. Every time you enter your office, notice the door and choose to center. At first this will need to be a conscious choice. Over time it will become a natural part of entering your office. There are millions of checkpoints out there. Here are just a few more ideas:

Telephone — When the phone rings, do not answer on the first ring. Pause and center. On the second ring, answer the phone. Whatever you say in your conversation, it will be from a more centered place than if you had answered on the first ring.

Computer — When you turn on your computer, there is usually a chime. Use that chime to center. One workshop participant wrote us, "Each morning when I turn on my PC, there is a note that says CENTER. It reminds me to get centered, and then my day begins on the right track."

Electronic car lock — One of our trainers tells a story of a workshop participant who centered every time she locked her car door with her electronic key. This was extremely helpful, as she often found herself growing irritated on her daily drive to work, and arriving at her office in a fairly uncentered state — not the ideal way to start a day. By centering at the beep of her electronic lock, she created the opportunity to begin her day in a calmer, more grounded state of being, something that I am sure her associates also appreciated.

Cry of a child — When your two- (or thirty-two-) year-old begins that whine which tests your ability to be a calm, loving human being, take a moment and center before you act.

A favorite tree or garden — Is there a place in nature that you pass daily which is pleasing to your senses? Consciously choose center as you enjoy its gifts.

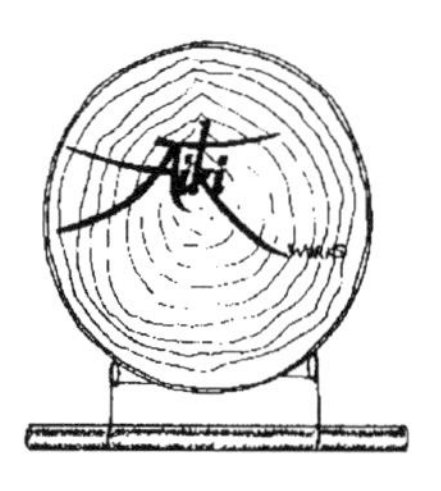

Centering Chime

What about a centering object for an entire group? Aiki Works produces a centering chime which our clients have found helpful in bringing a group to center. When rung at the beginning of a meeting (or when a classroom is losing its centeredness to chaos), the sound of the chime is an anchor for each person present to make a choice to center. This is different from signaling (or demanding) silence. The purpose is not to control the group, but to remind each person present to enter into a powerful, resourceful state for the upcoming activity. The chime, of course, can also be used by individuals as a checkpoint.

Key Words

A word or phrase can easily serve as a centering anchor — much the way a mantra supports you in journeying deeper into your consciousness. If you have some favorite phrases, try choosing center each time you hear or utter them. I often use the phrase "thank you" to look deeply into another's eyes and connect from center.

A favorite anchoring word for center in Aiki Works' programs is *yes.* A number of our ski instructors use it in our Magic of Skiing sessions to teach students to breathe and relax while they are making their turns down a ski run. As they begin each turn, the students yell out, "Yes!" The result — reduced tension, relaxation of breath, and lots of laughter.

If you play with this idea, after a while the words will elicit a centered state, much the same as the breath or a physical checkpoint can. In fact, there are probably a few words that are already programmed in this way in your vocabulary. Can you think of some?

Asking the Right Question

How can you turn an uncentered moment into a positive training? One suggestion is to recognize and embrace the moment, rather than denying it, and to immediately ask yourself, "What can I learn here?" In contrast, our knee-jerk tendency is to ask, "What do I need to say or do to be right?" This only leads us into an even less centered, hostile or defensive state of being.

Practicing the new question, "What can I learn here?" under stress leads you into what Thomas Crum calls the *Realm of Discovery* — a place of personal growth and peak performance. To the extent that "What can I learn here?" becomes your automatic response, you will experience a noticeable spaciousness in your life, and you'll gravitate toward a centered state.

Puja Dhyan, a trainer with Tom Crum, writes of a similar use of a question "It requires imagination to cultivate a richly expressive and meaningful life. Like working with a koan, one works with what *is* rather than with what you wish was. 'What's the gift?' is my constant question. It leads to deeper awareness and appreciation."

Resource Tip

The Magic of Conflict by Thomas Crum presents a full explanation of the Realm of Discovery and the Discovery model.

ENERGY EXTENSION

Energy is a natural physical force of the universe, present in all living matter. You have the inborn ability to expand and contract your own energy.

You are already familiar with the way this feels. Your energy is contracted when you are worn out, afraid, shy, or embarrassed. You may feel "shut down" or "two inches tall." Your energy is expanded when you are enthusiastic, proud, joyful, or in love. You might "glow" or feel "radiant," "on top of the world." In an expansive state, you feel boundless energy being generated within you and flowing through your body.

When energy is flowing freely through your body and you are in an expansive state, you are centered. Therefore, choosing to expand your own energy at any moment is a way to return to center.

You can learn to feel the level of your own energy and expand it at will. Once you are able to do this, many behaviors that you perform repeatedly throughout your daily life, such as driving a car, pushing a shopping basket or stroller, or typing at a computer can be a basis for centering training.

The Unbendable Arm exercise from *The Magic of Conflict* by Thomas Crum helps in understanding this process.[4]

With a partner standing by your side, extend your arm in front of you with your thumb up. Have your partner grasp your arm, one hand under your wrist, the other over your bicep. Allow your partner to bend your arm at a right angle to get a feel for the movement. Now attempt to be so strong that your partner won't be able to bend your arm. Many people make a fist at this point, modeling the conventional wisdom of brute strength. It is not important whether or not your partner bends your arm at this point (no broken bones please). What you should notice is the amount of energy and effort you have to expend on the task at hand — keeping your arm straight.

Next visualize something or someone important to you across the room. Imagine a stream of energy or laser light or water flowing from the fingers of your extended arm to the visualized person or thing. While you are connecting in this way, have your partner resume trying to bend your arm. (Your partner should do this slowly so as not to distract you.) Your arm should bend less than before, with considerably less energy on your part.

During the second part of this exercise, if your partner were to test you for center (as in the centering exercise on p. 8), you would be amazingly stable. This confirms that centering occurs when we are extending energy, letting it flow and expand outside of ourselves.

Resource Tip

Demonstrations of this exercise can be found on the following videos:
The Creative Resolution of Conflict (Aiki Works, Inc.)
The Magic of Conflict Video Seminar (Aiki Works, Inc.)
Violence: Dealing with Anger (Clearvue)
The Magic of Conflict Video Series (Career Track)

Playing with Energy

Select one daily activity, for example, brushing your teeth. Explore what it is like to do this activity different ways — with your arm limp, then rigid, and then with energy flowing. You will discover that, just as in the Unbendable Arm exercise, the activity takes less energy when you're in a centered state with energy flowing. If you perform the chosen activity with energy flowing, you are choosing a centered state, performing the activity with minimum effort, and taking another step forward in your centering training — all that while getting your teeth bright and clean!

Centering Moment

There are an infinite number of natural activities that lend themselves to centering through extending energy. Here are some additional suggestions:

Mowing the lawn
Walking the dog
Opening a door
Vacuuming
Washing your hands
Painting a room
Writing

Can you add some more activities from work? home? hobbies?

Expanding the Possibilities

As you explore the concept of energy flowing through your body, you are achieving a mind/body coordinated state that can be used powerfully in many activities.

Consider skiing. Think of an Olympic skier, in a downhill race or mogul competition, or landing after an aerial or ski jump. In all of these instances, the athlete's body is pliable, the epitome of energy flowing. You can apply the same technique in your own skiing. The next time you are on a ski run, imagine energy flowing endlessly through your legs. If you are a runner, you can use the same concept on your next morning run. How about swinging that golf club or tennis racket?

Sports are not the only arena for exploring this idea. Consider the simple action of getting up from a chair. Very often, we behave as though rising from a seated position is just that — getting up, moving in direct conflict with the laws of gravity. Instead, imagine energy radiating out of your body; when you wish to assume a standing position, begin moving from your center or hip area, forward and out (not up) to a standing position.

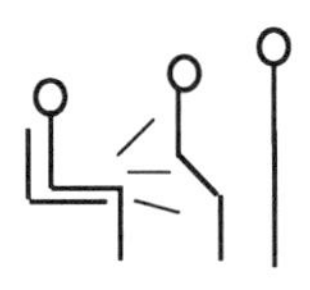

Centering Moment

What are some other movements that lend themselves to energy flowing?

Playing a musical instrument
Dancing
Walking in a crowd

Can you think of some more?

Ki Exercises

Ki is the Japanese word for energy. The martial art of Aikido encompasses a series of ki development exercises that everyone can use for centering training. These are described in several Aikido-related books (see bibliography). Here is an adaptation of one of my favorite ki exercises — perfect for subtle stress management while sitting around the office conference table, at a parent/teacher conference, during family dinners, or whenever you feel challenged.

Clasp your left hand with your right hand, both palms facing towards you and level with your collarbone. Your elbows should be bent. Lower your clasped hands towards your center, twisting and stretching your left wrist so your left palm faces to the left. Repeat in groups of five stretches per hand, alternating hands for each count of five.

As you perform this exercise, you should imagine energy flowing from your center, through your arms and into your wrists. Don't focus on the wrist. Direct your eyes out to the horizon. Scan your body for tension, and release the tension through relaxation as you repeat the exercise.

Resource Tip

You can see a demonstration of this and other ki exercises on the *Energizer* video listed in the bibliography.

The Gift of Touch

In my role as caregiver at a local hospice, the concept of extending energy has proven a gift not just to me but to our residents. So often, a simple touch with a conscious connection of energy flowing through my fingers to a resident brings peace to us both and a natural return to center.

The same experience has been true in my Aikido practice with the occasional injury. While others administer appropriate first aid, I can place my hands on the injured person, extending energy, creating an oasis of calm that helps the person to gain composure and deal with their pain or discomfort. It has also helped me to say the right words, authentically, without thinking.

Center is a place of compassion and empathy. It brings comfort when often the most important care you can give is simply to be there with someone.

**Our ability to center is a gift
not just to ourselves but to others.**

The Dance of Life

Combining conscious breathing, extending energy, and movement creates a wonderful way to train in centering. Pick a piece of music — a slow tempo would be best for starters.

Center and listen for a few moments. Begin to inhale and exhale in deep conscious breaths. As your breathing increases the flow of energy in your body, be aware of pockets of tension in your muscles. Stretch these muscles, moving to the rhythm of the music.

Give yourself a relatively open expanse of space so you can move freely, closing your eyes if you wish to focus upon your inner being. Listen to your body and move appropriately.

Enjoy — this is the dance of life.

Come now and join in the dance.
Ellen Stapenhorst

Theme Three: Reflection

Modern society breeds frenetic activity. From the moment we open our eyes in the morning, our senses are bombarded with stimuli. Alarms, traffic sounds, morning news, talk shows, kids fussing — all at once! And that is simply the start of the day. It continues in our cars, at our jobs, schools, community events, sports games. No wonder we find ourselves exhausted long before our bedtimes — exhausted and uncentered.

Creating time for reflection in our lives is one means to nurture centeredness. Reflection can take a number of forms, such as meditation, reading, or enjoying music. All create space within our frenetic environment where our spirit can rest and rejuvenate.

In allowing these moments, you will naturally enter a centered state. Here the discipline is to set up the proper environment. Once that is done, and you assume your meditative stance, sit back in a chair with an inspirational book, or do whatever it takes to begin your activity, your mind/body goes on autopilot. Centering happens. Your being knows the centered state. In fact, it has probably been waiting patiently all day for you to create its opportunity to seek that state. Could it be that some of our weariness at the end of a hectic day comes from a mind/body that is beginning to lose its patience and is simply tired of waiting for its time to center?

Reading

A trip to your local bookstore will reveal shelves of inspirational and personal growth publications. These range from books of quotes, e.g. *Earth Prayers,* to short stories, e.g. *Chicken Soup for the Soul,* to full texts, e.g. *Being Peace* by Thich Nhat Hanh. Pick a few of each variety and use them to help center your day. Tom Crum relates that every morning he crawls from bed to bathroom and begins his day with a reading from a book of quotes — an inspiring (and centering) start for sure.

You might also consider setting aside a longer period during the day for inspirational reading. I have found, for example, that retreating to bed maybe ten minutes before my spouse allows me time to read quietly. Gradually my body unwinds, my mind quiets, and my senses settle for the night. By the time I am ready for sleep, I am centered and far more able to drift off to sleep than if I had spent the time answering e-mail or watching TV.

Resource Tip

A must on any reading list are the basic texts on centering by Thomas Crum. Information on these and the other books mentioned above can be found in the bibliography.

The Magic of Conflict — Tom relates the basics of his approach to life and conflict resolution, which builds upon the art of centering.
Journey to Center — This collection of short stories teaches about centering through Tom's incredible real-life adventures.

Journaling

Quiet time spent recording your thoughts enhances your state of center. Have a journal available and use it at regular intervals. You may wish to set aside a particular time each day to record your experiences, insights, and dreams.

Entries do not have to be prose, or even written. Poetry, drawings, and other forms of expression all take us into a spacious, centered state of being.

A journal gives you a special place to collect breakthroughs in your perception and understanding of life's events and emotions. Keeping a journal slows life down and helps you to be present in the moment. Even if you never reread your entries, it doesn't matter from the perspective of centering training. It is the process that is of value here.

Resource Tip

Many texts on journaling are available. See the bibliography for a cross-section of selections.

Your Journey to Center — A Personal Journal (Aiki Works) is a beautiful resource for recording your thoughts. Quotes on centering appear throughout.

Music

What would life be like without music? Whatever your mood, there are tunes to enhance it. If you are seeking to create a centered environment, choose some music that supports you in winding down. Classical, jazz, or the full range of New Age selections easily fit the bill. A business executive sitting next to me on a recent flight said he always listens to Marvin Gaye; for someone else it might be Jimmy Buffett or John Denver. Once you have some tunes, create a space where you can listen without distraction — turn off the phone, shut the door — and then sit back and let the music lead you to your center. It is a powerful guide on its own, or as a backdrop to reading.

Resource Tip

Aiki Works has its own troubadour of centering, Ellen Stapenhorst. She has worked with Tom Crum for over a decade and is a singer/songwriter in her own right. Ellen's songs capture the essence of center and are an integral part of our residential workshops. Try her recordings, *Invisible Threads, The Dance,* and *All of My Skies* (see bibliography).

Meditation

In our residential programs, we begin each day with a meditation session. Usually about 20 minutes in length, these sessions are one of the purest forms of centering training.

There are many texts available on meditation. (See bibliography for suggestions.) Instructional classes in different styles are offered in most communities. Our purpose is not to advocate a particular form of meditation, but to acknowledge the power of this process in developing center.

To incorporate meditation into your centering training, resolve to make it a daily ritual. Assume that you will do so for at least six months before you evaluate its contribution. Rather than looking for earth-shattering changes during the trial period, consider whether the general tenor of your life changes. Are you, in general, aware of being more centered? Is there a greater calmness, happiness, or peacefulness to living?

Logistics

The logistics of meditation are simple. True meditation should be done in a quiet space. Listening to some relaxing music before beginning may be helpful. If weather permits, meditating outdoors is wonderful. A meditation by a flowing stream or river can be particularly powerful with the sound of the water carrying you in to center.

Meditation practice is not an effort, it is non-doing. It is a time to spend each and every day in that place inside yourself in which there is deep security and peace. It is really a letting go.

Thomas Crum

Choose a daily time of about twenty minutes to meditate. A traditional meditative stance such as seiza or lotus position is not mandatory. All that is required is that your legs be lower than your hips (don't sit on the floor with your legs drawn up), and your head be free to roll (don't lean against a wall). If you are seated in a chair, you may sit back, supporting the base of your spine against the back of the chair, as long as your feet touch the ground.

Once in position, begin your chosen practice to relax and enter deeper levels of thought. There are many options or vehicles for this process. Traditions as diverse as contemplative prayer, chanting, or simply sitting with awareness of thoughts all have the power to lead us into a deeper place inside ourselves. Tom Crum puts these various vehicles into perspective in *Journey to Center,* writing that "in all of these disciplines, the practice is not to force yourself into a state of peace, it is simply to acknowledge the mind's thinking nature and to relax into center so that you can settle down into deeper levels of thought, to the source of thought where the vibrational level is most powerful. It is achieving a place of deep connection and tranquility, where you are accessing a field of intelligence that is far greater than that derived from ego or intellect."[5]

If you do not already practice a particular type of meditation, you can seek support from groups represented in your area. Or, if you wish, you may try a simple technique such as the following:

Imagine a small version of you is sitting on the tip of your nose, observing your breath. Watch each inhalation and exhalation. Whenever you are aware of thoughts interfering with your concentration, bring your attention back to the breath.

Continue this process of observation, thinking, observation, thinking for twenty minutes. It is that simple. I have been following this simple form for many years. It has had a transformative impact on my ability to center.

Whatever meditation process you use, as your meditation period draws to a close, arouse yourself slowly. Don't just jump into the day's activities. Stretch, breathe, and resume your usual schedule gently.

When you first begin to meditate, you may need to set the timer on your watch or use some other means to signal the end of your allotted time. With practice, you will instinctively know when your meditation time has elapsed. Using a timer (preferably with a gentle chime) as a support eliminates the distraction of worrying about time from your meditation.

Some Thoughts on Thoughts

One of the most common reasons someone gives up on meditation is that they find themselves thinking when they feel they shouldn't. Being aware of thoughts does not mean that the meditation is not working — thoughts are actually the release of stress as meditation proceeds. The trick is not to get caught up in thoughts when they happen. As soon as you are aware that you are thinking, go back to observing the breath.

Jack Kornfield, a well-known author and meditation teacher, depicts thoughts or distractions as the natural movement of the mind.[6] When we begin meditation, our minds are far from quiet and settled; they are actively engaged in life. As we meditate, our minds gradually let go and settle, distractions cease to entice us. And, then, some tantalizing idea or memory arises and the mind awakens to savor it. The key to meditation is to view these distractions as waves, to welcome them, and to seek the calm between the waves. As each wave passes, return to the quiet, settled space that allows you to journey deeper within.

All of man's troubles stem from his inability to sit quietly in a room alone.

Pascal

Walking

Taking a walk is a time-honored means for reflection. A stroll along a beach or a hike in an ancient forest center us naturally through their peace, beauty, and energy. However, it is a trap to assume that scenic beauty is a requisite for a reflective walk. I grew up in New York City, walking three city blocks every day to school, along a concrete sidewalk, past an asphalt playground and vacant lots. Not exactly the Grand Canyon, yet I can still relive the way my mind transformed those surroundings into the perfect setting for a centered walk. How? My childhood inquisitiveness took in everything — city sounds, faces of passersby, tiny green plants eking out an existence in those trash-laden lots. My mind would journey vast distances during that daily trek and, in truth, those morning walks were a favorite part of my day.

You can turn any walk into a centering experience, simply by getting present with the moment, taking in your surroundings, and breathing from center. In this way, a simple trip to the copy machine or the library becomes an excursion in centering. Don't wait for special surroundings to make your day special.

Centering Moment

What activities or moments in your day offer you a moment of center? There are probably a number which are an oasis of peace amidst the daily bustle of living. How about a hot shower, a clerk in a coffee shop who always greets you warmly, the fragrance of your spouse's perfume or aftershave?

Stop and appreciate what these moments contribute to your day. If you appreciate them more fully when they occur, their centering effect will extend beyond the moment into the rest of your day.

Letting Go

As my personal centering practice develops over the years, I sense a growing place of calm and reflection within my being. When I'm tuned in to this place, I feel a sense of peace no matter what is happening around me. I can gain perspective on any situation and compassionately witness my behavior and that of others. When I experience tension intruding upon this reflective space, I have come to look upon it as a signal, a red flag, telling me that I have more to learn in the discipline of "letting go."

"Letting go" is often discussed in the Magic of Conflict approach. We speak of letting go of our positions on issues long enough to get a real understanding of opposing views. In beginning an actual conflict resolution process, the likelihood of a win/win solution increases with a letting go of attachment to particular outcomes.

In this usage, letting go relates to your inner self — your attachment to beliefs, processes, people, even your self-image. When you enter deeper and deeper into a reflective space — whether through meditation, music, or simple awareness — the areas where you still need to let go become dramatically clear.

What does this process look or feel like? For me, there is a nagging discomfort, an unsettling feeling. It saps my energy, interferes with my reflective state. I've come to recognize that it usually means I am interfering with the unfolding of the universe, trying to manipulate life to fit my preferences — holding on, rather than letting go.

For example, as I age, I find myself clinging to the wish that I were as physically resilient as when I was younger. The training

---

To center is to relax the tight fist of clinging.

Thomas Crum

is to honestly face these attachments when I feel the discomfort they create, and to explore what it would be like to let go of my need to control and to possess. What would it be like if I simply experience what *is?* My body is aging. How can I nurture its present state rather than longing for the past?

Since, for most of us, our attachments in life are many, this approach provides endless training opportunities and a pathway to greater center and power. It isn't just the major issues and events that challenge us to let go; the practice of letting go is equally important with life's little trials and tribulations. Why won't this traffic move faster? Why can't we change our meeting format? Why won't my child pick up her room?

I have found that when I do let go, I am able to focus on the positive, to enjoy what *is* good in the present moment. I may not be able to make the traffic speed up, but I can use the time I am stuck in traffic to listen to that audiotape I've had in my car for the last two weeks, or better yet, spend a few minutes on my misogi breathing.

As you let go of attachments, vulnerability emerges. One of our Aiki Works trainers, Ellen Stapenhorst, shares this story of training with Terry Dobson, a great American aikidoist, shortly before his death in 1993.

> The last few times Terry was out here in the Bay area, he was in various stages of severe physical illness. Here was this big man, so used to being in charge, at least of himself, barely able to walk on his swollen feet and breathe with his clogged lungs. Yet, he still stepped onto the mat. And now his question was, "What do we do when we are totally weak and vulnerable? Where is our power in this condition?" And we practiced total surrender, being totally present in our vulnerability, embracing our weakness. And we discovered, in those rare moments of approaching surrender, a quiet strength that was irresistible to the attacker — the power of facing and choosing our own death. In some ways, this was finding an ally in the black hole as well as in the sunburst of dazzling energy which we tend to prefer. The down side is part of life, and there's wisdom in it.

It is important to remember that while "letting go" may feel scary to anticipate, it is the opening to a powerful and joyful life.

Centering Moment

Close your eyes and breathe deeply. As your body and mind quiet, reflect upon your attachments in life. In what areas do you need to let go? What would it look like if you did? What one small step could you take today towards that greater freedom of letting go?

Theme Four: Vision

Vision is inextricably woven together with center and power.

Centering increases your ability to stay focused while heightening your awareness of all that is going on around you — but it is hard to stay focused without a vision.

At Aiki Works we define true power as energy flowing freely towards a vision. Without a vision, it follows that it is difficult to be truly powerful. You may have lots of energy, but without vision, your actions can be likened to an inflated balloon releasing its air, randomly darting in various directions. Ever been there? We all have.

How often do you reflect upon your vision in life? What about in the various circles of your life — home, school, work, church, hobby? Can you crystallize your reason d'etre so that it is there, present, to inspire you when times get tough and you have difficult choices to make?

Where there is no vision, the people perish.
Proverbs 29:18

Defining Vision

Vision is a compelling, engaging, vivid picture that inspires you and moves you to action. To work on defining your vision, create a centered space, much as you would for a period of reflective time. Choose a medium for expressing your flow of thoughts — the written word, sketches, music.

Next, center yourself. Take some deep breaths and allow your body and mind to relax deeply into a peaceful place. Visualize the various aspects of your life and perhaps choose one to focus upon, such as your vision for yourself as a parent. Ask yourself, what is my vision? Ten years from now, when I look back, what will I want to be able to say about my parenting? If there were just one gift that I could give my children, what would it be? Express your stream of consciousness surrounding these questions through your chosen medium. A journal would be an excellent place to record your thoughts.

During this process, give yourself time to explore the various answers to your questions. Do some resonate more than others? Notice if one theme begins to predominate in your answers. Look for responses that capture qualities that exist outside of form — as a parent I will give honest, truthful guidance, or be a model of giving and receiving love freely — rather than focusing upon specific outcomes such as helping with homework or attending athletic games.

If you find yourself stuck on specific outcomes, keep asking the question, "If that happened, what would be the result?" This questioning process will lead you into qualities that transcend time and material possessions. If I attend my child's basketball games,

---

Getting clear about your vision takes some deep thinking and feeling. It's not always easy or immediate, but just keep contemplating it and eventually clarity will happen.

Thomas Crum

what would result? She would know I care about her participation. If that happened, she would know I am interested in her life. If that happened, she would know that I care about her, and she would know she is loved.

Visions at this level are what will support you in times of conflict when you are searching for inspiration to take the right action. What do I say to my eleven-year-old when she misses a key basket in a championship game? Knowing that my vision is to have my child feel loved is likely to generate a more compassionate response than is a vision that focuses upon specific ways to support my child in achieving greatness as an athlete or scholar.

Take time for this process of defining vision. Don't rush to get the perfect answers. Be patient if in one sitting you discover no particular clarity. This is a process you can return to again and again.

Repeat this process for each area of your life — relationship, parenting, career, your role in your community or church, your vision for yourself as a whole. See if your individual visions have a common thread — a unifying theme. Gather your symbols or sentences together in a journal for future reflection. The outcome — a clear understanding of your priorities in life — is then there to support you in times of stress and decision.

Resource Tip

The bibliography lists a number of excellent sources of support in understanding the vision process.

Revisiting Vision

Vision renewal — revisiting and refining your vision — is an important support in centering training. Unfortunately, in corporate America at least, developing vision statements often falls short of its potential impact. A work team might gather in a retreat setting for two or three days and develop a common vision. But, after the retreat, back on the job, life goes on as before, with vision statements tucked away in binders or retreating towards the back of a shelf.

The benefit gained from defining a vision is only the tip of the iceberg. The real value lies beyond — in using your vision as a means to regain center under pressure and stress. This is available to you only if you revisit your vision often enough for it to rise up to your consciousness when you need it.

The process of vision renewal does not have to take place in a quiet, distraction-free environment, though daily reflective time is an excellent opportunity for reviewing your vision. It can be as simple as noticing what is your vision for yourself as a parent while you watch your child playing. Or as you commute to work, appreciating the real reason you are engaged in the "rat race."

Soon these snapshots of your vision or purpose will become second nature to you. When life is in turmoil and you ask, What am I doing here? Why can't I just run away? Your vision will rise to the surface, quickly and clearly, inspiring you to hang in there.

Centering Moment

Post a key phrase or drawing that embodies your vision in a place where you will see it daily — on the refrigerator, your office wall, or the dashboard of your car.

Regaining Center

Once you are in touch with your vision, your awareness of incongruity between vision and action will increase dramatically. And if you choose center in those uncomfortable moments, you will be unable to deny that incongruity. What then?

First, be gentle with yourself. There is a saying in conflict resolution circles, "be hard on the issue, soft on the person." Action out of line with vision must be acknowledged and altered — the sooner the better. It is important to appreciate that this will happen faster and with greater ease if you are compassionate with yourself. This is a challenging task, to say the least, for you are your own worst critic. Remember, beating yourself up for some inappropriate action is off-purpose, often self-indulging (we all know how to wallow in our "stuff"), and takes energy away from the best course — moving back on track with your vision.

Second, value the process of instant replay. What would it have been like if you *had* acted congruently with your vision? Visualize this possibility. This is actually centering training. Your mind takes the replay in as well as if it had actually happened and learns a better choice. Next time a similar situation arises, the chance of a centered choice is higher as a result.

Finally, be aware that incongruity between vision and action may be a signal of the need for change. Is it time for a change in career, relationships? Or does your vision need some rethinking? The answers to these questions may come only slowly with time for reflection. All that is certain is that clarity will be more accessible from a centered state than an uncentered state. Remember to ask yourself, What do I need to learn here?

Theme Five: Support Systems

Do you know your own support system? Moving through life is difficult enough; to do so without friends and resources is next to impossible. Even the solitary soul has a support system. It may be a pet, a special retreat spot, a precious book that re-centers. Support systems are more obvious for some than others but we all have and need them.

To train in center takes support. The choice to center is your personal choice. Support systems strengthen your ability to center in times of stress.

Possible supports include a circle of friends or a group that shares your interest in centering, or anyone who increases your ability to be centered, whether they're interested in centering in a conscious way or not. You can also seek out workshops which allow you to renew your skills and explore new applications with guidance from trained facilitators. You may also learn an art such as tai chi chuan, aikido, or yoga, in which centering is a core skill.

It is in the shelter of each other that the people live.

Irish Proverb

Daily Community

No one lives in a vacuum. Each of us is part of a community which extends beyond the people we see each day to friends and family in faraway places.

Carolyn Shaffer and Kristin Anundsen speak of "conscious" community which "nurtures in each of its members the unfolding from within that allows them to become more fully who they are."[7] In other words, conscious community supports us in being our centered best.

Take a moment to evaluate your personal community — the network of people you come in contact with on a regular basis. Do you see your community as supporting you in your centering growth? Are there some members of your community who positively reinforce your centeredness, providing you with positive feedback and appreciation when you are centered? For example, I have a friend that I am in touch with almost daily. We simply touch base with each other, listen for a few moments to the other's crises, and then offer encouragement. Short, simple, sweet, and very centering to us both.

Communications technology such as e-mail allows us to gain a great deal of support from people we rarely see. We might have friends we've never met! Members of the Windstar Foundation began an online newsgroup a few years back. Intended as an electronic means of conveying information on environmental issues, over the years it evolved into a close-knit group of friends following each others' lives while promoting environmentally responsible community action.

My insurance policy is my friends.

Jan Thomas

If you consider your personal community lacking in its ability to support you, how can you develop a support network? The options are many — renew old friendships, join an established special interest support group, or become part of a service or religious community where the focus is positive. Remember, people don't have to understand the concept of center to support you. What is essential is that they appreciate you when you are at your centered best, and ask the right questions when you are uncentered to help you regain your equilibrium.

Resource Tip

Creating Community Anywhere (Shaffer and Anundsen) is an excellent reference on community building. See the bibliography for more information.

Centering Arts

Eastern culture has been steeped in mind/body training for centuries. There are many disciplines, such as yoga, tai chi, aikido, and qigong, which emphasize movement and attention to center, providing a natural forum for developing awareness of center.

For example, consider aikido, a relatively modern martial art begun in this century by the Japanese martial artist Morihei Ueshiba. Aikido is an art of self-defense with an intention to de-escalate conflict situations. When attacked, you move off-line of the attack, harmonizing with your attacker's movement in direction and timing. Aikido requires movement from center in a way that destabilizes the attacker and defuses the conflict.

Similarly, in arts such as yoga or tai chi, appropriate movement requires centeredness. While center also supports appropriate movement in most sports and many other arts utilizing movement, the centering arts are unique since part of their purpose is to develop center, so center is recognized and often discussed. In sports such as skiing, tennis, or golf, only the rare instructor consciously encourages centering. I have often said to my students that there are few places comparable to our aikido dojo where you can find a community explicitly designed to help you learn to handle stress more effectively.

Life on the Sahara

Maybe you live in an area like the middle of the Sahara Desert, where there appears to be no instruction in any of the centering arts. You do still have options — there are many books and tapes available in various disciplines. While nothing replaces a live instructor, you can gain much value from these resources. And perhaps you can get to an occasional workshop for personalized study. Also, look for classes in sports, music, art, or any other field where a teacher is especially aware of center.

Workshops and Retreats

While daily practices are at the core of your training, there is an advantage to taking time, as your life permits, to get away from it all to rejuvenate and renew your skills.

Evaluate your life. How much time can you take: a weekend, a week, a month? How often — biannually, or perhaps once, twice, three times a year? What is your budget for personal growth work?

With this basic information, you can begin to choose some options. Decide upon the format that works best for you. There are retreat centers across the nation and around the world that offer varied classes. Perhaps you find the writing of one author particularly intriguing and you would like to learn more from him or her. You can usually contact authors through their publisher or on the Web. Often you will find they are offering programs.

View these programs as gifts — opportunities to immerse yourself in your own personal growth. It is the best centering training you can ask for. And, often, you will discover centering supports to help you when you return home to daily life — resources, improved skills, and networks of people to stay in touch with.

Resource Tip

Aiki Works offers a range of workshops which include centering work within the context of conflict resolution, skiing and golf:

Beyond the Gold
The Magic of Skiing
The Magic of Golf

Part Three

Putting It Together

Your Personal Training Plan

Centering is your choice. It is as simple and as challenging as that. You have the ability within you to change your experience of your life. That is incredible if you stop to think about it! No waiting for Bruce to grow up, Marsha to stop drinking, graduation, that promotion, or early retirement. The ability to live a fuller, more loving life resides within you now.

In this book, I have presented an array of activities that enhance and deepen the centered state. Any of the suggestions within the five themes can help you to strengthen your ability to center. It is now up to you to craft your own personal training program.

As you flip back through all the suggestions, you'll notice that a range of training possibilities exists. Some tips take little preparation to implement (you can probably identify two centering checkpoints you can begin using the minute you lay this book down). Other suggestions require more — a bigger time investment, perhaps some organized initial training (for example, studying with a meditation teacher). Some suggestions are daily practices, others are occasional. There are also different levels of training. Choosing unbendable arm while driving a car requires a different level of discipline from the challenge of letting go of attachments in life.

The message is again that there are many paths to center and many ways to train. All are valuable and all bring you closer to a deeper and more powerful experience of the centered state of being. The choice is yours.

To craft your personal plan, review this outline of suggestions made within this book. Prioritize activities that resonate with your center. Go back and reread the sections on these suggestions. Add your own thoughts, recording your choices in a journal.

The Breath

- Misogi Breathing
- Breathing Moments
- Choosing a Smile
- Getting Present in the Moment

Reinforcements

Anchors

- Checkpoints
- Key Words
- Asking "What do I need to learn here?"

Energy Extension

- Playing with Unbendable Arm Movements
- Performing Full-Body Activities with Energy Flowing
- Ki Exercises
- The Gift of Touch
- The Dance of Life

Reflection

- Reading
- Journaling
- Music
- Meditation
- Walking
- Letting Go

Vision

Defining Vision
Revisiting Vision
Regaining Center

Support Systems

Creating and Appreciating Community
Practicing Centering Arts
Attending Workshops and Retreats

In developing your plan, keep these guidelines in mind:

Variety — Select activities that you wish to explore further from across the five themes. For example, don't simply decide on five checkpoints or energy extension activities to comprise your entire training program. The five themes together formulate a balanced approach to centering training.

Intensity — Vary your level of training. Choose some simple, fun tips and balance these with some requiring deeper commitment. For example, resolve to incorporate a breathing moment of your choice into each day and to attend an intensive workshop once a year.

Balance — Be prudent in the number of activities that you choose. In my aikido classes, I often watch students come in and with great enthusiasm begin almost daily practice. Too often, within a few weeks they burn out and drop out. In contrast, students who begin with commitment but pace their involvement practice many years.

As you develop your training plan, choose activities that you can realistically incorporate without overwhelming yourself. Appreciate that some suggestions do not add to your schedule, but transform the way you perform exisiting activities. Let balance be your guide in your choices.

Commitment — Once you have selected activities, commit yourself to following through on them for at least six months. Remember it takes time to repattern behavior. If you persist in your training, change will occur. What you are starting is a lifetime process.

Create some cards like the ones shown below to summarize specific ideas that appeal to you. Place each card where it can serve as a frequent reminder of your intentions — on a mirror or bedside table, in a favorite book or your purse.

Tips for Getting Centered

- **Enjoy slow deep breaths.**
- **Let go when things don't turn out as I'd hoped.**
- **Center when the phone rings.**
- **Meditate daily.**

Tips for Getting Centered

- **Stretch and smile.**
- **Center as I punch my time card.**
- **Attend aikido class twice a week.**
- **Practice misogi breathing.**

The Path Beyond

I am only one,
but I am still one.
I cannot do everything,
but still I can do some things.
I will not refuse to do
something I can do.

Hellen Keller

The impact of centering in your life will be experienced in many ways, in many arenas. My personal experience, and that of many who have passed through our programs and continued training on their own, confirms this.

Centering can be there for you within seconds of unexpected crisis. Writes one program participant:

> Around 10:00 a.m. I went walking down Madison Avenue in Manhattan. As I dreamily and disconnectedly walked along the street, two very large men came up beside me, pressing against my shoulders like two bodyguards.
>
> I did not have my normal "wary traveler" guards up — handbag under coat, etc. Instead my shoulder bag was outside my jacket and suddenly it felt much lighter.
>
> I looked down to see the flap open and my wallet gone. The two men and I were continuing our threesome along the street. I kept walking and looked from one to the other realizing that one had my wallet. I centered and turned to the man closest to my bag and said, "Excuse me; I have just lost my wallet. I am an Australian in New York. I am on my own and my wallet has everything I need — my passport, credit cards, airline ticket, and money." The man looked at me and handed me back my wallet! I thanked him and the two walked off.
>
> To this day I am unsure if it was my Australian accent, the sheer honesty of my request, or the calm (stunned!), polite way I asked for the invaluable wallet.

Centering can support you in more planned events, such as those uncomfortable but necessary events in life like visiting the dentist. Michael Lewis, a dentist who also teaches Magic of Conflict workshops, suggests:

> If you are facing a dental visit and your normal response is fear, find yourself a quiet place, relax and get centered. In your centered state, cue on a scent, sound, or object and make it your anchor. At your visit, center, remember your anchor, and extend ki as the assistant leads you to the treatment area. After you are seated, re-center with your hands folded just below your navel. Breathe! Extend ki to your caregiver and trust the process. It will be a different experience.

John Phillips, one of our Magic of Skiing instructors who broke a leg one winter, suggests centering for physical therapy:

> Become centered while at physical therapy. Centering brings you more in the present. You become much more aware of your body and its movements. You can perform the exercises properly and isolate muscle movements. Centering also changes your relationship to pain. Is this necessary pain to work through or are you pushing too hard?

Another area of application of center is professional performance. We have heard this from many of our own trainers and workshop participants. Centering can provide the clarity to take action:

> I came into work, ready to start the day. By 8:30 a.m., I found myself moving the stacks and piles of papers on my desk from one place to another. All of a sudden, it hit me — I was feeling overwhelmed. I realized I needed to get centered so I could think clearly.
>
> So I stopped for a few minutes, took some deep breaths and got centered. Then, I consciously thought about why, at this particular time, I was feeling this way. I asked myself what in this situation was within my control. The answer was, what I chose to work on as a priority for that day and how I chose to view this situation — as something awful or as a challenge to be more efficient and more focused on my work. I also decided to meet with my manager about priorities.

Centering can also impact upon the attitude of others, as I witnessed at a conference in Ireland set up by an American group:

> Imagine 1,500 conference participants, predominantly American, descending upon a town of 13,000 inhabitants in rural western Ireland. The town, while a tourist mecca, still had to stretch to ac-

commodate. As might be expected in any large gathering, some logistical problems arose — seating arrangements and other particulars often left something to be desired. As the week progressed and people sat listening to presenter after presenter, they got more and more "into their heads." As mind and body disconnected, attendees were increasingly uncentered in expressing their distress with the town, the hotel, and the conference volunteer staff.

The result was conflict. And I was intrigued and impressed by the Irish delegation's means of handling the matter. By midweek they had organized, processed, and made a statement before the group on their feelings — that the conference was being held neither "for" nor "with" them but *"on"* them. Their group presentation modeled "hard on the issue, soft on the people" — something that had not necessarily been happening at the conference — and with their statement, something shifted in the conference. The logistical problems didn't disappear, but everyone showed more understanding of the Irish, and their feelings as unofficial hosts.

Real healing came with laughter on the last evening. A dramatist from San Francisco did a "Saturday Night Live" style stand-up comedy routine on the conference. Interspersed with poignant vignettes on rainforests and other topics, she addressed every quirk of the conference from food to conference seating, much to the delight of the audience and the hosts, who were also present. Stress was released with each uproarious laugh. In the end we left with a much healthier perspective on the logistical problems we had experienced and a better ability to appreciate the true depth of our experiences.

The benefits of centering can show up in the most surprising places at the most welcome moments. A few years back while heli-skiing in the Canadian Rockies I discovered this:

As the clouds rolled in and visibility declined, we descended to ski at lower altitudes in a compellingly beautiful pine forest. Beauty aside, for me skiing through those individual trees that made up that forest was challenging. In fact, skiing 2,000 vertical feet of those trees was a feat of Olympic proportions. On more than one occasion I felt my center leaving, or more precisely retreating uphill — a no-no in skiing, where the object is to move with gravity, not against it. My dear guide Hans pointed out, "You must go down, Judy, there is no other option." He was right, of course, and infinitely patient, but it was not that simple for me, since I had contracted myself to the size of a snowflake.

By the end of my first tree run I had shifted into one of my favorite uncentered themes, "beating myself up for not being good enough." Help! Now where was that Magic of Conflict stuff? Could it really work in Canada? And could I remember enough to regain my center before that helicopter returned to take me back up for another run in those trees? Fortunately, I was surrounded by so many kind people genuinely wishing for me to have a wonderful experience that I was able to focus and draw upon some deeper place in myself to find that lost balance. I realized that the quality of my experience was my choice. My next run would be influenced more by my mental attitude than my skiing abilities, which were definitely sufficient. So I centered, breathed deeply, and next thing I knew I was back up on top facing the same forest of trees. This time, though, I paused to center every time I felt myself drifting off (or up) on the way down. And, no great surprise, my skiing improved dramatically and I was able to go back to enjoying the aroma of the pines and the majesty of their numbers as I danced among them.

Centering is your ally in finding balance when events truly beyond your control overwhelm you. One such moment for me was the bombing of the Federal Building in Oklahoma in 1995. The extent of death, injury, and destruction challenged my sensitivity and balance greatly:

Watching the chaos at the bomb site, the mangled bodies of the children, my center, my balance faded. Anger and frustration overwhelmed me. I wanted to blow up the people responsible; to deal in "an eye for an eye." Yet, even while I was accepting this darker side of myself, I was aware of its incongruity with my more usual self. Part of me simply witnessed my negative feelings and emotions, asking quietly, "So, do you really want that?" It was as if my "better half" was dancing with my darker side, stepping back, acknowledging the force of my outrage and leading me patiently back to center.

In the days immediately after the bombing all I could do was witness the emotional roller coaster welling up inside me — empathy for a now childless mother, cynicism with the analytics of a spokesperson with an ax to grind. Not only did I witness my own emotions, but also those of others paraded before me on television. Anger, blaming, name calling; grief, agony; commitment, dedication; numbness, shock, passivity. Those who were centered in their feelings touched me deeply. With others I experienced an incongruity similar to my own.

As the tragedy played on, I began to ask, "What can I learn here?" and to search for some threads, some pieces of a framework to lend some sense to the wreckage before me. That process supported me in regaining my own center.

The difference between those reacting versus responding to the bombing was immediately clear. Reaction is uncentered, at the mercy of a situation, similar to losing one's balance from a shoulder grab attack in aikido. Victims react to conflict, upset, tragedy. In contrast, those who are able to maintain center when attacked can stay connected with others and operate out of a higher place of vision and purpose, with compassion. The responses of these people inspire others to action, soothe pain, and create hope in the midst of death and destruction.

As the days wore on, centered responses began to emerge. In our community, schools and civic groups began to raise money for victims, write letters to survivors, plant gardens in memory of the deceased. I participated in this. Reaching out was a healing process and an important transition. Victims are helpless, and feel unable to act. Resuming movement, action, allowed me to regain control of my life, reestablish connection, and deal with my fears.

Centering also can be an ally in facing that final conflict that we all share — death. Like many others, I spent years avoiding, not embracing, death. Hospice workers write of the peace and deep transformation that they see experienced as death approaches and is accepted. I have witnessed this myself. Rodney Smith in *Lessons from the Dying* suggests that if we were able to accept our mortality earlier in our lives (a process that most definitely requires a centered state of being), the power released by that acceptance and letting go would be available to us sooner.[8] Sometimes it takes a life-threatening event to accomplish this. For me, this was true. A brush with cancer clarified for both my spouse and me what our priorities and vision in life were. The years since that scare have been dearer for us because of the perspective it taught us. I thank centering for allowing a potential nightmare to be transformed into the basis for a deeper relationship.

Fire is hottest closest to the source and our biggest tests of center are naturally with those closest to us — parents, children, spouses. I began my conscious practice of center twelve years into my marriage with two small children. Centering radically changed my relationship with my family. It has created many priceless scenes and teachings, and enhanced my ability to appreciate them:

- A seven-year-old's truthful feedback that Mom wasn't being very centered over a sibling's outrageous behavior.
- Coping with an adolescent's query, "Can I dye my hair blue, Mom?" from the spacious place that it would eventually grow out or fade away and there were many worse possibilities (though not many rivaled the prospect of taking her to my in-laws' fiftieth wedding anniversary with blue hair).

- The opportunity to swallow my ego over my parenting skills, which I had often taught in our school district, when our junior high principal called to report that the apple which launched the biggest food fight in the history of their cafeteria was seen in my son's hand shortly before it started flight.

Ah yes! Life's been quite a journey and training grounds for center. I've learned much, laughed, cried, and felt eons and eons of gratitude for the opportunities life has given me — and for the gift of the art of centering.

Good luck to you on your journey!

References

[1] *The Magic of Conflict,* Crum, Thomas, p. 55, Simon & Schuster, 1987

[2] *Being Peace,* Hanh, Thich Nhat, p.5, Parallax Press, 1987

[3] *Being Peace,* Hanh, Thich Nhat, p.5, Parallax Press, 1987

[4] *The Magic of Conflict,* Crum, Thomas, p. 89, Simon & Schuster, 1987

[5] *Journey to Center,* Crum, Thomas, p. 75, Simon & Schuster, 1997

[6] *A Path with Heart,* Kornfield, Jack, Bantam, 1993

[7] *Creating Community Anywhere,* Shaffer, Carolyn and Anundsen, Kristin, p. 11, Tarcher/Putnam, 1993

[8] *Lessons from the Dying,* Smith, Rodney, Wisdom, 1998

Bibliography

Inspirational Reading

Aikido in Everyday Life, Terry Dobson and Victor Miller (North Atlantic, 1978)

Aikido and the New Warrior, Richard Strozzi Heckler (North Atlantic, 1985)

Being Peace, Thich Nhat Hanh (Parallax Press, 1987)

Chicken Soup for the Soul, Jack Canfield and Mark Victor Hansen (Health Communications, Inc., 1993)

Earth Prayers, Elizabeth Roberts and Elias Amidon (Harper Collins, 1991)

How Can I Help?, Ram Dass and Paul Gorman (Alfred Knopf, 1985)

In Search of the Warrior Spirit, Richard Strozzi Heckler (North Atlantic, 1990)

The Intuitive Body, Wendy Palmer (North Atlantic, 1994)

It's a Lot Like Dancing, Terry Dobson (Frog, 1998)

Journey to Center, Thomas Crum (Simon & Schuster, 1997)

Lessons from the Dying, Rodney Smith (Wisdom, 1998)

Love Is Letting Go of Fear, Jerry Jampolsky (Celestial Arts, 1988)

The Magic of Conflict, Thomas Crum (Simon & Schuster, 1987)

Meetings at the Edge, Stephen Levine (Anchor, 1989)

Peace Is Every Step, Thich Nhat Hanh (Bantam, 1991)

The Tibetan Book of Living and Dying, Sogyal Rinpoche (Harper Collins, 1992)

Meditation

The Art of Meditation, Joel S. Goldsmith (Harper Collins, 1956

Breath Sweeps Mind: A First Guide to Meditation Practice, edited by Jean Smith (Tricycle, 1998)

Journey of Awakening: A Meditator's Guidebook, Ram Dass (Bantam, 1990)

A Path with Heart, Jack Kornfield (Bantam, 1993)

Ki Exercises

Aikido and the Dynamic Sphere, A. Westbrook and O. Tatti (Tuttle, 1984)

Children and the Martial Arts, Gaku Homma (North Atlantic, 1983)

Ki in Daily Life, Koichi Tohei (Harper & Row, 1978)

Ki: A Practical Guide for Westerners, William Reed (Japan Publications, 1992)

Journaling

At a Journal Workshop: Writing to Access the Power of the Unconscious and Evoke Creative Ability, Ira Progoff (J. P. Tarcher, 1992)

How to Keep a Spiritual Journal: A Guide to Journal Keeping for Inner Growth and Personal Recovery, Ronald Klug (Augsburg, 1993)

Dear Diary: The Art and Craft of Writing a Creative Journal, Joan Reubauer (Ancestry, 1995)

Journaling for Joy, Joyce Chapman (Newcastle, 1991)

A Voice of Her Own: Women and the Journal Writing Journey, Marlene Schiwig and Marion Woodman (Fireside, 1996)

Your Journey to Center: A Personal Journal (Aiki Works, 1999)

Community

Creating Community Anywhere, Carolyn Shaffer and Kristin Anundsen (Tarcher/Putnam, 1993)

The Different Drum: Community Making and Peace, M. Scott Peck (Simon & Schuster, 1998)

Music

All of My Skies — Ellen Stapenhorst (KiNote Productions)

Ancient Isles — Richard Searles (Earth Dance Music)

Celtic Twilight — (Hearts of Space)

The Dance — Ellen Stapenhorst (KiNote Productions)

The Four Seasons — Itzhak Perlman and the Israeli Philharmonic Orchestra (EMI)

Invisible Threads — Ellen Stapenhorst (Beechwood Recordings)

Mysterious Mountain — Alan Hovhaness (Delos)

Pangaea — Stephen Bacchus (Oasis)

Relaxing Interpretations of John Denver with Nature (Nature Quest)

The Sky of Mind — Ray Lynch (Windham Hill)

Something Constructive — John Jarvis (MCA)

Ten Years — Kitaro (Geffen)

Videos

The Creative Resolution of Conflict, Thomas Crum (Aiki Works, 1984)

The Energizer, Thomas Crum (Aiki Works, 1987)

The Magic of Conflict, Thomas Crum (Career Track, 1996)

The Magic of Conflict Video Seminar Kit, Thomas Crum (Aiki Works, 1991)